BONE HOUSE

POEMS

Scott Laudati

.BONE MACHINE, INC.

First Edition

ISBN: 0692056513
ISBN-13: 978-0692056516

BONE MACHINE, INC.
14 Allen Avenue
Manasquan, NJ 08736

www.BoneMachineBooks.com
ReadBoneMachine@gmail.com

Edited by: Christina Kaylenhart

Printed in the United States of America

also by SCOTT LAUDATI

.poems.
Hawaiian Shirts In The Electric Chair

.novel.
Play The Devil

DEDICATION

Carlos Gonzalez
Thom Young
Caitlin Burke

Three heroes who've listened to way too
many of my 3 a.m. conspiracies, but still
pick up the phone when I call. Thanks.

CONTENTS

something like love.

i miss you,
blue eyes.
lying in your
bed
while you walked
across campus.
looking at
jersey mountains
rolling away from your path
like the sleeping stomachs
of giant buddhas
and me staying
warm,
making the bed
so we could unmake it.
using your roommate's
teapot to bring
your small bones back to
life.
and your soft skin
under my heat.
"it could be love," you said.

you hate me now,
blue eyes.
you used the

bruises of your old
lovers to build back
something more
and i let the
past leave me
with less.
i could see
no dark spots
in you
but my pain
needed company,
and when once
you thought
love could conquer,
by our epitaph
your eyes
held the ruin of
an idea
abandoned.
"it could've been love," you said.

who are we now,
blue eyes?
i've erased
the words and the doubt.
i only remember
how your cat ran away
every time i opened the door
and even though

your dad was
a cop i tried
to like him anyway.
we had no vices then.
we could go
to the zoo sober
and smile at turtles
and pet the zebras.
that last time we
drove all night
i reminded you of
those turtles
who seemed to smile back
and we rolled
and kissed
and ignored our sins
and once again
we talked about
forever.
i always try and
go back to
that night i let you
get on the plane
and you left me
and new jersey behind.
"it can still be love," i said.

i always try and go back to that night.
in my mind.
in my songs.

because it
was something like love.
we
were something like love.

leave me alone.

you're the new guy
so you work the graveyard shift.
the boss has finally gone home,
you can smoke a cigarette in peace.
no hiding
no sneaking around the corner.
the garbage trucks clean up the streets.
you watch the last of the drunk girls
stumble out.
some go home alone
some fight with their phone.
the city is finally yours.
just a faraway hum of an ambulance.
no taxi horns.
no one is left to ask anything of you.
the soft gray clouds reach
over the low tenements
with winter always right behind them.
and the bums
sit against the brick walls
like tomorrow is guaranteed.
and they know your face,
they can see what the job has done
so they don't lift their cups,
just a slow nod or nothing at all.
the same as last night.

and you keep thinking the world
is going to end
but right now that
doesn't make you feel so crazy.

alone.
finally.
over rats
and cobblestone.
it's a world
that failed a lot
of people
before you showed up for a paycheck.

buffalo bones.

an unsmoked cigarette
burns for thirteen minutes
without a drag,
and since you're all grown up now
there must be a wedding day.
the town will throw you a parade,
rope off the streets where tanks
have rolled
and teenagers did *the hokey pokey*
after sunday mass.
they'll re-introduce you to the
man who baptized you,
he says the lord's prayer often
but it doesn't
sound familiar.

the blimp banner clocks the national debt
but nothing about all the i.o.u.'s
for last month's rent,
or how fast cigarettes burn
as you sit around counting hours.
an arc of time is never real until
your lover pulls the joker.
you're all in, full ante,
and one hand later
the game is over.

you know it then.
they lied to you but that's okay.
it just hurts real bad
when the rules change
and your professors
still want the homework.
maybe santa will pay the late fees
if you say grace every day of lent.

pull out the old box of maps
from under your bed.
get your revolver loaded and
pick a direction,
a spot on the map
you've never been before.
hitchhike to the dakotas
where the weather's colder.
where strangers with no faces
stand over your shoulders
counting pages in your notebook.
the wolves run free
no swings in the park.
maybe the buffalo jumped the cliff for fun,
left their bleached white skulls in the pits
looking up.
they're hidden until the thaw.
that's when you'll find them grinning
with the spring bloom.
don't worry,

eventually
we all shiver
in the sun.

if i could go back
i'd change everything.

it's been a little
while since
i took the
typewriter
out.

i've
moved
on, i guess.

another girl.
a different time.

those keys
she cleaned
one by one
they don't
work so well
since i threw
it
out of
my window.
i don't know how
it missed the

taxis and the tourists
but it
didn't even
bounce.
it
just sat
there
staring up at me
until i went
down and picked it up.
it's a hex
on my heart
that chills
like a cat
or a guinea pig,
offering nothing,
but i still try and
feed it my soul
sometimes.
and now most
of the keys
refuse to move
or they
jam.

i know
it's
a broken

machine
but sometimes
on nights
when i'm feeling
brave
i'll try
those keys
again
and when
they cross and catch
i'll arrange the
letters
in different
patterns
hoping
there's a message
there,
a riddle
that will lead me
back to her.

you can see
why typewriters
fall like
anvils
from my window.

coast to coast.

my real education
began
after college.

i moved to philadelphia
to record
an album with marcel
and for two days,
before any recording
was done,
we drank black coffee
and
we listened
to coast to coast am
on surround sound.
i already knew
our parents
our teachers,
they were all reading
the same script,
pre-approved
and designed to keep
us fat and middle-class.
but poor marcel had been sheltered,
there was no dissent
in his blood,

no older brother ever
forced him to listen
to punk rock.

it took twenty-four years
but david icke
and alex collier
finally showed him the crossroads -
that moment when
you know know for sure
they've always been
lying to you.
you either go on
voting
and obeying them forever,
or you head for the basement
and start thinking
about revenge.

marcel was the
craziest guy i've
ever met
and sometimes
during recording
he'd cut the music abruptly
and run to the window,
convinced he had
just seen
a spaceship.

at the time
this seemed normal.
marcel had a pre-birth
vision
of being in a room
and picking out his parents.
a humanoid race
somewhere in the stars
had sent him here.
but the mission had failed him
like it had failed
everyone
and he wanted
to go home.

we were kids then,
full of guts
and heart,
scared of everything
and ready to
fight our way
to that place where
it all evens out.
our youth was
bulletproof.
but they
were all worried
about my friend
marcel

and when he
got too worked up
over aliens
and reptiles
they sent him away.

i remember holding my friend,
telling him no
matter what
we were up against
we were in it together.
but we live in a time
where you run on the wheel
or you get committed.
and i'll always
wonder if my
encouragement gave
him the confidence
he needed
to break.

i saw him months later,
medicated and confused.
he said
he wasn't sure
about anything
except that
after high school
he'd go home and

stick his
trumpet up
his ass while he jerked off,
and he was afraid
nothing
was ever going to feel
that good again.

time won't save us now.

i sit above
them at my
desk and look
down at the bars.

all the bars,
all with
400 ipa's on tap
and 80 imported bottles.
and they come
from parts of the
world i used
to dream about going
but it seems
impossible
now that a place like
prague actually
exists
and you can go there if you want
and the people there
are sitting
and drinking
just like you.

and when i think about prague
i feel like they

just *know*
and they never
feel the tension.
they can
sit and drink
and waste time
because
they can't fall far enough
to bypass pity.
they'll never know
american blame.

and they scream
downstairs
and fight
and the girls cry
into cell phones
at men with
good haircuts
and boating shoes
and tucked-in polo shirts.
they rule my city now.
and they follow the
girls and
promise them something
i can't.

in
new york

it doesn't matter
if you
can dress yourself.
a good haircut here
costs $150
a week.
in a city
where no one drives
that says
the same
thing
about a man
a maserati does
somewhere else.

and
it still
says
the same
thing
about me.

a prophet.

they were parents
from the suburbs
and they were scared
of new york.
she was fat
in her neck
and her knees
and he had his socks
pulled up to his
fanny pack
and i thought
"if this was new york
in any other era
they'd be picked clean."
hell,
i might've even done it.
they just looked so
weak.

she was yelling
at her husband over
a map.
they were lost
they were afraid.

i saw him come

out of the subway.
no shirt
maybe two teeth
and as he passed me
he smelled like
the corner of every
subway station -
the real cooked
and dried piss
that climbs
into your nose
like a razor.

the bum walked up
behind them.

"what should we do?" the fat lady
asked her husband.

he pointed at a chipotle,
but before he could answer
the bum leaned in
and said
"burn your bodies."
then he clutched his hands
around the husband's waist
and laughed, "make sure
you leave them
well-done."

it was the first time i thought
maybe there *was* someone
on the other end
of that telephone
all the crazies
seem to be on.

and they were getting pretty
good advice.

he never was one
for conversation.

he was straight edge
until
twenty-one
and six months later
they found him
in his backseat.
od'ed
for the
second time.

my best friend.

but he wouldn't die
even though
they seem to
so easily now.
he tried.
he kept
his demons
close
and just as
his eyes
started
to shut out the light
they would step in.

no retreat for
my friend.
they wanted just enough
of him alive
to keep
feeding.

it was his birthday
i remember
that we got him to drink.
twenty-one
years and we
undid it
with a bottle
of johnnie double black.

i was always
one of those
who could do the line,
smoke the pack,
and then
wake up
with nothing
in
my head
telling me "just
one more".
but i never had any trouble
with living,

and i think that's
more rare
than a kid
twenty-one
who's never touched
booze.

and six months
later i was
on line
with a
couple dozen
black mothers
and their kids,
waiting to see those
that hadn't done
any worse
than anyone else,
but in a country
that makes everyone
a criminal
we were waiting
to see the ones
who got caught.

the guards pushed mothers,
called little kids
"animals" right
to their mothers'
faces, and when they

got to me,
the only
white kid
in line, everyone
just looked confused.
i was a part of
their world now
and
neither team wanted me.

my friend had followed
the junkie script.
he robbed his
brother's kids
and pawned all
their toys.
and so dope sick
with nowhere to find help
he went right to the corner,
right for
the needle.

i don't know
what his mother's
face looked
like when she
found him
full
of puke

or when she sent
him to jail
but
i remember
my mother's face
the first time the world
made me cry,
when
she realized
she
couldn't save me anymore.
it probably
looked something
like that.

it was my turn eventually
and i got to see my friend.
he was a man now,
heavy
from the weights
and
the bologna sandwiches
and blue milk.
and so pale.
the same dull color of the walls
he now called home.

the phones
were broken

so we had to bend over
and talk
through a little slit
in the glass.
i couldn't really hear him
but his skin
was so pale
and he said more than
anything,
his loss
of respect
and freedom,
they took
the sun from him.
he said
that's what life needs
and even if he
couldn't change
who he'd been
at least under
the sun
he could grow
and maybe someday
bloom.

i walked out of prison
and touched
every tree

and thought about
the signs
and the bad moons
and my friend
who went to sleep
and came back
under the same
fluorescent lights.

the squirrels.
the car horns.
the mail man.
it was like staring at
a diseased mirage.
but they were free to be nothing.
so i stared
and i was grateful.

sit with me.

can you sit with me please?
i'm ready to tell those
stories you should've heard
before
i made you
unforgiving.
i've written them to you now,
in each letter -
pulled out
put down.
you know
the ones? two stamps
in case my feelings become too
heavy.
another weight
i don't mean to make you carry.
can you sit with me please?
i can put us onto paper
now, more than this
loneliness
more than this regret.
i can lock us in love
i can lock us in time.
we can be in old books on a shelf.
used and traded and passed
back and forth,

and put a smile
on the face of all those
who come after us.
what if we could make their world better?
i can't do it without you
i can't.

i wish this didn't happen.

remember when you got the guts
to tell me
i'd never be happy?
while you were crying
and naked
waiting for me to understand
what you already knew?
it was the moment
i realized
i'd always be alone.
i said you were crazy
but a better man
would have called it
bravery.
i can remember your diary
on the floor
lying like a bone,
the inside of you
showing itself to me.
you weren't an artist but
i'll bet a younger you
wanted to be.
and i remember i
only had a hoodie for
the walk home.
the smoke trailed out of

my mouth
from your front door to
my back porch.

the time after that
when you took me back
you asked me
"why can't this
just be easy?"

i wanted you to understand
it was never meant to be
that way.
we were just actors
playing characters
on a cold stage.
no notes
or method
or clear understanding
of why the curtain
always falls
exactly
the same way.

we were born under the same moon.
shared the same bad sign.
and it worked for awhile
because you saw life
for what it could be

and i saw life
for what it was.
but there's no peace
for people like me.
all those hours you spent
smiling in your sleep
i knew *they* were closing in.
so i never slept.
and i wondered about
my home in the sky
or my hole
in the ground.

i hope you know
what i know now.
that *they* were closing in for you.
but it wasn't
to take you.
they built a wall around you
that showed itself sometimes.
when light fought its way
through leaves and
windows
and under doors
like carpets
to warm your feet.
it was never easy
because i never
had faith in anything.

i was just like the rest of them.
and i loved you
because
you weren't
like any of them.

i forgot about all that.
and light was always around,
i just never noticed
until it stopped
shining on us.

an everyman.

he ran the grill at
every family bbq
and wore the same
cargo shorts and mets t-shirt
each time.

he hated mexicans.
he hated liberals.

i made a mistake once
and said i wanted
to go to thailand
in front of him.

"thailand?" he said.
"why
would anyone
go to thailand!?"

i named a bunch of things
but he really focused
on the beaches.

"beaches?" he said. "you want
beaches? go to myrtle beach.
they've got crab cakes.
you can walk on the sand,

stick your toes in the water."

he was an idiot
but everyone liked him.
they liked him way more than me,
especially when
the burgers were done.

he noticed i didn't take one.

"i don't eat meat," i said.

"you don't eat meat?" he asked.
"best trip
i ever took
was toronto. 1978.
i had a steak the size of a baby.
only time i ever left the country.
thank god."

i told him about my trip
to toronto.
i couldn't afford food
but i ate molly
every day
and swam in the lake
with golden retrievers
and blonde women
who floated on their backs

like vacationing angels,
giving the seagulls
a reason
to keep circling.

"it might've been
the best time
of my life," i said.

"best time of my life was
the 1962 world series," he said.
"hands down. i was six
and watched
the game every day
with my father.
i knew i could do
anything after that."

his greatest achievement
was someone else's victory.

maybe i would never
have a best moment
that trumped all the others,
but i hope the
best ones
are like the worst ones,
and when i look back
there'll be too many to count.

remember to make sure
your accomplishments
are yours.
the failures as well.
those will always
be more important.

everyone hates you.

everyone hates you.
even if you haven't figured it out yet
don't worry,
you will.
it'll be the confirmation of your biggest fears.
your father saw something better.
your readers thought there
was promise.
but they were wrong.
anyone who has ever
believed in anything is wrong.
even after you put your grandfather
in the ground,
after the speech about how you
used to sail around
the swamps of eastern maryland
and put chicken in crab traps to see
what kinds of turtles
swam in for the flesh,
you'll be wrong.
about how he was your hero once.
you were wrong.
and then your aunt will find his diary
and you'll read that he was like everyone else.
that he thought you were born
with all the promise

and yet you wasted it
on a stupid major,
on the women you followed
like a new gospel,
and all the forgotten words in your notebook
that never amounted to a decent novel,
that you would fall further
than your privilege should've allowed.
and you'll think about your appetite
and how it far exceeded your talent.
and you won't fight back
because you'll know
he was right.

buying cocaine for **** *******.

i was just about to quit for good.
it was another day carrying bags
up and down stairs
while guests stood
in front of the elevators
and complained that they
were taking too long.
guests who had just gotten done
bitching about the lobby,
that the air conditioning
"was too cold",
that new york had
"too many rats".

usually i skipped the elevators
and hoofed it up the stairs
with their luggage strapped
to each shoulder.
it gave me five minutes without them.
and if they'd already pissed me off
i might accidentally
drop their bags a few times.

i wouldn't even wait for them
at their rooms.

it was the same story every day.
they had no cash
or they only had euros
or they would pretend
to forget my tip altogether.
but that night i didn't
punish the bags,
i just left them on the floor
and decided
"i'd rather be homeless".

there were always windows
you could open
and step out onto fire escapes
for a quick leap,
or empty rooms
with fresh sheets and
high rafters.
but that night was the first time
i realized you could just walk out.
it wasn't against the law yet.

i thought about it on the way
down the stairs,
and i probably would've done it
but then i saw *her* in the lobby -
a famous actress i'd had a crush on
since the days
we bought tickets for

singing animal movies
and then slipped into
the r rated theater
when no one was looking.

i grabbed her bags but i didn't
take the stairs,
i stood right next to her
the whole way.
"how's your day going?"
she asked.
"terrible," i said. "i was just about to quit
and then you walked in."
she smiled.
i had said the right thing.
i couldn't believe it.
i looked back at my coworkers.
they couldn't believe it.

when we got to her room
i asked her if she'd ever been
to new york before.
of course she'd been to new york.
hell, she was the girl i thought of
when i thought of new york.
but she laughed.
everything that came out
of my mouth was stupid,
but it was coming out right.

"what else do you do?" she asked.
i told her i was a writer.
"what are you working on?"
"i just had a book published," i said. "would
you read it?"
"a real book?" she asked. "sure."

i kept about 30 copies of my book
in a locker
downstairs for just this reason.
i went to get one
and there was some crisis
in the lobby.
my manager asked me for help
but i shook my head.
there was more at stake
than keeping my job.

when i handed my book to her i said,
"they're poems, but they don't, like, rhyme."
she gave me a $10 tip
(the most i'd ever been paid for my writing)
and i left,
wondering about this world i had entered,
always surrounded by
fame and money
and none of it ever crossing over.

we never had a lunch break

at that hotel,
you just left
whenever you wanted
and when you got bored
you went back.
this was down on ludlow street
so i walked to the cake shop
and ordered a budweiser.
it was happy hour and the bartender
slid two in front of me.

i was pretty drunk after
an hour of that.

my phone was buzzing the entire time
but i ignored it.
when i got back the girl
at the front desk jumped up.
"where have you been?"
"working," i frowned.
"*she* called down!" the girl said. "*she* wants you
up in her room."

i rode the elevator looking at myself
in the reflection
of the brass doors.
this was my moment.
she's read my book, i thought.

she's going to take me away from
all of this.

her door was open when i got there.
a guy was sitting on the floor
strumming a guitar.
he wasn't good.
she introduced us and i could tell
by his indifference he was some
la kid,
born rich,
and all he had to do
was be at that right club
on the right night
and now she was his.

"you're a great writer," she said. "that's why
i need your help."
i was a bellman,
i would get fired
if i didn't do what she wanted,
and usually, this meant
i would get arrested
if i got caught.

"i need to finish a script,"
she said. "can you get me a bag?"
i swore i'd never do it again,
but what the hell?

"how much
do you want?" i asked.
the guy with the guitar was
finally interested.
"get two," he said.

she handed me $300.

it was a new hotel and
i'd never bought coke
in that neighborhood before.
janis was my favorite cocktail waitress
and she was running
the lobby bar by herself.
but janis was a soldier.
i told her what i needed
and she left her customers and
took me to another bar.
"i know a guy
with the best coke," she said.

i looked at her nose.
i watched her inhale a cigarette.
janis had a beauty that ran so deep
all her hard work
couldn't betray it.

she took me to max fish and
her guy charged $100 a gram.

that was a crazy price
and the bag looked really light
but janis had done me a solid
so i gave her $50
as a thank you.

when i got back into the lobby
ben stopped me.
"we've got to try it out,"
he said. "you can't give
her a bag of shitty blow."
we went up to the manager's office
and did a bump.
then another.
"never forget," ben said, "they're paying us
to snort this right now."

i went up to her room and
she opened the door, drunk.
"do you have a dog?" she asked.
i knew she was one of the
adopt or die types
so i said "yeah" but
i didn't elaborate.
she told me a whole story
about white people
and how they're the first
ones to get rid of their dogs
when times get tough.

"i hate everyone," i said. "people
don't deserve dogs."
she liked that.
she took the coke and kissed me
on the cheek.

the next day she told me
she was getting an apartment
around the corner.
it sounded like an invitation.
"i'm leaving new york," i said. "why do you
only get the girl
after you buy the plane ticket?"
the la guy parked a convertible
against the curb.
"that's too bad," she said. "it
could've been fun."
then she walked past me
and threw her suitcase
into the backseat.
she blew me a kiss as she sat
in the passenger side
and put her feet up on the dashboard.
"it could've been fun," she yelled.

the staff looked at me,
waiting for an explanation,
so i gave it to them.
"all the poems in the world won't buy you

a convertible," i said. "i don't know
how many times
i have to learn that lesson
before i stop
trying."

the woolly mammoth.

remember back when you were young?
you thought you'd get a diploma
the old-fashioned way.
the first voice of a new generation
screaming "get me out of here"
or "i want to go home".
i heard it down hallways
before we rolled dice
on the bathroom floor.
i heard it like a slave hears
new religion raining from the trees.
from homeroom to the principal's office,
they tried to take it out, arrest your rage,
but it stunk up every vein in your body
like a clogged sewer,
and you were never afraid to lose it.
"in the womb," you told me once,
"i was unhappy even then."

and then there were the streets.
the bus station in newark
and the park two blocks down
where the runaways raid
the pigeon coops and
they find dead bums
and cigarette butts dragged out.

it was like a vacation home right on a river,
under buildings like dead peaks so the sun
never shined into your eyes.

it was so you,
every move planned for the great story.
those were the days you were always
looking forward to.
the envy of every fool.
you wrote your own legend
and it kept me amused.
i used to think that was pretty cool
but i'm invisible now,
i'll fade away
like the woolly mammoth
but you …
you'll live on forever as
some kind of cinderella,
or a pin-up girl.

the basement days.

his parents
let us smoke
in their basement
and we played music
and drank all night
and pretended
we were asleep
while his dad
got ready for work.
and once he left
we'd start painting again
until the very last
dark corner
of the window
was taken by the sun
and then we'd collapse
in exhaustion.

time always against us.

i can't remember
what the rush was then
or where the drive
came from
but we
never looked

at those four walls
and the
warm heater
and the tea
his mother made us
with anything but
fear.

fear
of those parties in brooklyn
we weren't at.
fear of a whole life
in front of us
and missing
a single cobblestone street in
a world that wasn't
too big yet.
a fear i can only
see on my dogs face
when i say "i'll
be right back".
the unknown
the missing
the *what will we become?*

we left
that basement
as fast as we could.
left the suburbs

for landlords
who won't let us
smoke inside.
and now
it's just bars.

to face your life
in the mirror
of a bar bathroom
again
and again,
it's just too big.
we had a basement
and tea once.
we were tremendous
and the world
outside the door
was small.

smoking and painting,
just waiting for a sunny june
to finally live all the plans
we'd made in winter.

we were giants once
and the world
was small.

the good fortune execution.

sometimes i think we are like flowers
so fragile
reaching up from a hard cracked ground
shivering shoulder
to shoulder
waiting to be ripped apart
in the endless storm
like old dirt praying for rain
begging for just a drop
show us *something* is up there
and that *something* cares.

they fill the headlines with
the ones who need
god the most,
lined up against the wall,
blindfolded.
some get it quick
some get lucky.
the good fortune execution.
no dirt
no planes overhead while the kids
shake back and forth,
hands around their own throats
praying to die.
what a silly god.

he always enjoyed a good show.
and the real headline grabbers
don't end in a sentence,
those kids choke to death in real time.
but god doesn't read the newspaper,
or maybe he does and he just hates the
poor and the weak
the same as everyone else,
only maybe
a little bit more.

because he does smile on some.
and the chosen ones
thank him
in their speeches and
over their steak dinners.
wouldn't you?
this world was only made for the rich,
and just because they don't show it
doesn't mean they don't know it.

but the poor have to live here, too.
and while we watch hope fade
like a plane
headed for the horizon
sometimes it's hard to remember that, yes,
we have to live in this country
but we don't have to love it.
and like every other boss i've served under,

god would do a lot better with a
bullet in his head.
and those under him,
crawling on all fours in his shadow,
saying
"yes sir", "no sir",
saying "yes please", and "thank you",
should share a similar fate.
or maybe something worse.
no blindfold
no execution.
just the curse
of spending eternity
in his company.

right after high school.

we drove around egging cars
when joe la first got his license.

i'd come home at 5 a.m.
trying to sneak in before my father
got up for work
but i almost always got caught.
and he'd say the same thing
every night:
"life is passing you guys by."

one night we egged the wrong car.
we were at a stoplight and
a guy pulled up in a big truck
and in the passenger seat
his girlfriend looked over at us,
a car with five idiots all staring back.
we rolled the windows down
and i popped through the sun roof
and we all fired our eggs.
probably thirty eggs broke
against the guy's car.
then the light turned green
and we took off.

he chased us

but not like any of the other chases.
this guy swung his car at ours
and missed by an inch.
then he handed his girl a gun
and she pointed it
out the window at us.

we ran the next red light
but he went through
right behind us.
joe drove the car in an s formation in case
the bullets started coming,
and finally he pushed the throttle
to 120 mph
but we couldn't lose the guy.

we all knew we were going to die
and we all knew we deserved it.

in new jersey
the jug handles
are on the right side of the road
and you need to take them
to do a u-turn.

joe went into the left lane.
the guy changed lanes
and got right behind us.
maybe two feet before the jug handle

joe cut the wheel.
we swerved across three lanes
and clipped the exit sign.
the car went up on two wheels
and we came back down hard
but joe never lost control and he
never slowed the car down.
the guy in the truck hit his brakes
and tried to drive
through the intersection
to head us off
but a minivan came across right then
and broadsided him into the divider.

we were all raised catholic
though none of us believed in it
and we probably should've
thanked something,
maybe the rest of them did,
but i just rolled a joint in that silence
and then we drove to 7-11
and smoked it
in the parking lot.

my dad was in the driveway
warming up his car when i got home.
"my friend's son is getting his master's
degree. he's going to be a teacher,"
he said. "none of your friends

71

will ever do that."

he was right,
they wouldn't.
but joe la had just cut three lanes
at 120 mph with a gun
to his head.

no master's degree
could teach someone how to do that.

i went in and slept until
my father got home from work.
that night joe la picked us
all up again
but we just went bowling.

believe it.

there's a mirror on her dresser
with old polaroid's wedged in the sides
from a time when love was new
and we thought the 60's could come back
and the fuzz from the camera's old filter
looked like something holy
surrounded our world.

she curled her straight hair
in the glass and it held
while she put on a new dress
and even though it's new york in august
she can always find a tree in harlem
standing over the last breezy corner.

she doesn't believe in fairy tales.
i never did either.
but here we are
at central park and it's midnight.
and once again there's a girl
i find myself planning a future with
telling me what can never be.

it's always like this.
and tomorrow will always be like that.
confused. hungover. broke.

checking my wallet to see
if i still have a metrocard.
and always surprised
that i slept so well
while the pigeons meditated on wires
and she called out of work.

medal of valor.

you stop drinking
stop smoking
stop traveling
stop cocaine
stop seeing your friends
stop fighting in bars
stop the weekends
stop sleeping
stop taking the train after 11 p.m.
stop making it
stop eating meat
stop talking about the universe
and they stop judging you
because you're just like them now.
and your age shows
when you're in a crowded room
because the one kid
who didn't stop
has the girls
has the friends
has his youth
and you realize when it's too late
that the only crime is fear
and you folded
with a royal flush
because the other players

kept a straight face
while they were playing
a weaker hand.

there's always food
for a fool and his money
but the king still sits
at the head of the table.

the heart of america.

i lost another one who didn't want love
or forever
or some way back to
the heart of america.
she just wanted kids.
white kids
named john and jesse and little sally.
kids that would get her off work
and never make her think
about california
and giraffes
or the way she felt at 16
when her parents stopped loving her
but said the words anyway,
who looked at their little girl
and decided she didn't have *it*
so they went to the next one.

she wanted kids who'd adopt a dog
named lady or molly,
and a vet who might say "it's 1/4 pit bull
but the dog will never stop looking like a lab".
and the house could be new.
and the kids would never have
their own minds.
they would be patriots

and they would never fail like citizens.
their mother could change the truth
and never have to explain
that she'd found love once
and it didn't act
like it was supposed to,
that she didn't say "hit me"
while age and time were still on her side.
the kids would never want to know
about the heart of america
and that it disappeared
just around the time that
they made it cool
to sell love
for money.

the twilight's last gleaming.

it's not funny
i'm not hungry
i wish i died before the 90's came back
but no one retires at the right time.
the fade is a slow burn
and usually the ones who
could've been good
drop out first.
they name baseball fields after them
probably a scholarship
but no one alive cares,
memories replaced too soon
by the next draft.
and no ghosts hang like frames
in these halls,
the dead don't want any part of this shit
either.

no one is well.
the fast clap of the audience was
muted long ago.
the people needed to eat and
stole the generator.
the nypd shot at the black ones
and the white working class
didn't like it this time.

no one is well.

they turn the lights on
but the audience doesn't laugh.
the twilight last gleamed on
some other era when we
didn't have to hide
from the dawn
and everyone could still smile
at the mirror.

the oath.

we slit our wrists to the side
and put them together
and you told me your father
had been murdered
as our lines crossed and nothing
internal knew no boundaries.
we didn't die like i thought we would
and you spread our blood around your face
like war paint,
two checks under your brown eyes.
i tuned my guitar and you danced naked
like a shaman
while i strummed an old folk song.
my parents were looking for a second house
in florida
and i forgot to feed my mom's fish
and the dogs thought we were insane
but we were happy.
and in the kitchen
we lied down
like we owned the floor.
and we bled together on my mom's new tile
like love
burrowing into the earth.

when i see a pair of ducks

flying together to the ends of the map
i think of you, the one who gave me
more than her heart,
the one who
opened herself up.
and even though we didn't make it
to the end of the earth
i slept well and
i woke up in a better world.

from my window.

the bad reviews came in dozens this time.
i stacked them around my altar
two high
and looked out my window at
the george washington bridge.
would they call me too white
if i did a cannonball
off the upper level?
do they know what it's like
to write a novel?
have they ever sat
with their notebooks while
words fell onto the page
like spears from the heavens?
what neighborhood can you live in
when you need time to type a masterpiece?
the bosses want you there at 7 a.m.
rain. shine.
immaculate conception.
do nothing and have it appear.
major in education
take the civil servant test.
time runs out
time runs away
time
time.

it gets to be too much.
did the poet's parents tell him to get a degree
before moving to the village?
did they buy art from the store and leave
plastic stretched around the frame?
how do they know i'm not bob dylan?

the fallback plan eclipses the dream.
die broke with
a blank passport and no epitaph.
give them what they want.

i watch the intersection under my window
and i think
this could be so easy.
go to maine and buy a copy of uncle henry's
at 7-11.
barter for a rifle.
polish it on the greyhound home.
spend the weekend
setting up a perch in my window
while a new hit song about losing
her virginity sings
to me from the stereo.
percolate a strong cup of black coffee.
step out into the morning and fire
a few warning shots in the air
like davy crockett
on a deer blind.

watch their feet run around
the sidewalks like ants
dodging a magnifying glass
until finally the pack separates and
one runs right into the cross hairs.

boom.

there are many ways to be remembered.
just hit one.

skinned knees.

emmy doesn't hurt here
like she did in the poughkeepsie pool halls
when the boy she liked couldn't wait
so he went for the easy kill
and her friend took the bait
and no one seemed to pay any price
when the sins were tallied up.
the rule book says scissors beats paper
but never rock,
and emmy wasn't always sure about love
but
her faith was enough.
she started as a kid with dirt in her cleats
and graduated to high school
before she skinned up her knees.
even when the winters came
and the rivers iced up,
emmy wasn't like all of us,
she was never at her worst.

the winnebago boys met us for wings
one of those frozen new paltz nights.
they brought their guitars and a harmonica
but while they were tuning up
a pitcher broke and
somebody's girlfriend took a fist to the floor.

the boys ducked out back
before the dust cleared
and we saw their winnebago
skid down main street
just as the cops pulled in
and drew their guns on
everyone in the parking lot.
conor oberst bought them new shirts
and we watched them all on tv one night
in your new place.
everyone was always running away,
but not you emmy,
i could count on you to stay the same.

i remember the spring
and how the snows melted around
your broken town.
the rivers rose up and the
warblers headed north.
there was no sun in
your basement apartment
when the apples grew in the orchard
but even with all that dark
sleep was still tough,
so we started stealing your mom's
klonopin before lunch
and eating them for dessert.

you were always praying for heaven

because life is hell,
but our love wasn't,
and god may have failed you
but the music will be better down below,
and you know all our friends will be there
so we'll never have to
go home after last call.
we'll finally have time to be ourselves
and no one will ever care that we spent
our whole lives
pretending to be everything else.
emmy doesn't hurt now
emmy doesn't hurt now.
she stopped counting on the scales
to balance themselves.

a life.

i used to walk around and look at alleys
or hidden corners of parks
and think,
when i've finally lost everything
i can be homeless here.

but then i got older and
left new york.
i drove through appalachia
and the sad and stalled midwest
and finally made it to
montana,
where the wheat was so healthy
it was almost gold,
and no money
had ever talked to the land.
it had escaped the experiment.
it remained free.
i saw myself as a successful writer looking
out over that grass and thought,
someday when i've had enough
of this awful world
i can kill myself here.

and that's why i leave
instead of just signing the lease.

it's hard on the soul to stay.
i hit a new city like a camera
and memorize everything.
and once i've drank in all the bars
and had coffee in the morning
it's time to run.

it's the same conversation every time.
with my girlfriend
with my mother,
that it's nothing
they did,
i just never learned
to take life
as it comes.
there's never been a past,
it's all new to me.

maybe you know what i mean.
i've looked at women
with the old soul eyes,
who've stood on this dirt before,
and they know for sure
this is just one life
and so it will be again.
but not me.
i clocked in with clean lungs.
a boy that learned fear
that became too sad to cry

that didn't know
there would be a second chance.

always remember,
if there's nothing left to lose
run for the finish line.
always remember,
it's the fight of the century every time.

always remember,
death
will be easier.

i remember you and me.

i was the last one to turn
seventeen so i never
drove to her house,
but she picked me
for a season
and the driver never looked up
when i walked onto the school bus
and we rode together to
the other side of town
when her mother
was at work.

i was too lame then
to understand
what that meant
but it didn't stop her
from bringing me up the stairs
to her bed.
usually we spent those days kissing
but one time she cried.
she told me about another boy
and i felt something i never
had before. i took a sharpie
and drew a heart
on her hip
and told her

as long as she kept me
i would treat her heart
like it was something i could see.
i'd never be like them.
i wouldn't pretend
a young girl didn't need
to be kissed goodbye
or that she wasn't holding me
like it was the first time
every time.

my friends would pick us up
before her mom came home
and we drove along
the navesink as the leaves changed
and the horses hung their heads
over the fences.
the front seats were pushed
far back and i remember her smile
as i put her legs over my knees.
i was still young enough
to see a future in her smile,
i didn't know other girls
could look at me like that.

a few years later they lowered her
into the ground
wearing her mother's pearls.
i watched the priest from across her grave.

in a tie she would've
hated me wearing
i felt something else
i never had before.
looking at that priest i knew
in my heart i could kill.
when he said
"this is god's plan"
i wanted someone
to squeeze his throat
and scream
"your god did this
and now he gets her?",
and when no one did,
i wanted it to be me.

but then i saw her mom and i understood.
i could only stay silent because i had loved her.
if i was god i would've taken her, too.
the world is very bad company and we didn't
deserve her. when you write a perfect song
you don't give it away
you keep it for yourself.
we knew it
god knew it.

his plan made much more sense to me
once i figured that out.

your sunday best.

i can see girls at barstools
ready again to push their doubts
down past the breakers,
past spilled pints and men
that wouldn't carry them on their backs
like their fathers.
there are cities and towns all over
this country filled with families
saying grace and eating dinner.
and no one knows
why we shake hands
and leave mass promising to be good
to each other.
you can trace the line up the tree
but the sidewalk splits once you walk
through the door.
everyone surrenders
and the cars drive home.
a black flag flies where america once
stood.
there are killing fields in the backyards
full of fresh wounds and broken hearts
and around here
we all bleed the same.

no future.

they laugh at me at weddings
at reunions
at the 7-11 and probably
in the backyards where we used words like
best friends
and *someday.*
i'm their jester now.
the one who puts it on the line
for their amusement.
like drinking in these caves is easy,
like i wanted to put down words on paper
that didn't resonate with anyone.

it's open season on the weak.
the waitress
the deli girl
the ones who write poems
in their own blood
and give them out for free.
should the naked be hunted
just because they walked outside?
don't look for sympathy in the smiles,
it's been a gamble
since the first amen.

i know this was all for nothing now.

i should've listened to my father
back when there was still
an exit off this road.
back when i wanted to live much longer
than i do now.
back when i felt the fire
and lived like it was never going to
burn out.

ruined.

it was one of a kind i thought back then,
and it happened
just in time.
i didn't turn out like
the others
who missed
out on a young love
and spent their 20's obsessed
with finding it.
i knew it existed
and i knew
i didn't want
any part of it.

you did it to me
and i didn't understand
until years later
how much i owed
you for this lesson.

we took long walks at night around our town
looking in windows at wagging dogs
and lizards under lamps.
and i knew
that those lizards dreamt
of more heat

and in those long winter nights
so did i.
i dreamt of your heat
under clothes
under red hair and pink skin,
under blankets i felt so trapped
but i never
took them off.
it was your heat.
i wanted it to
suffocate me.

and one morning we both
woke to a song bird
sitting on your father's flag pole.
"it's looking for a lover," you said.
and i knew i'd found mine
so i said that.
i said "i love you".
and you
weren't as sure as me
but you said the words anyway.

we stopped
those nighttime walks
when we
became a couple.
we caught up on every season
of every show

and at night
i didn't sleep
quite so close
because i had you now,
i didn't need to suffocate anymore.

and one afternoon
when your parents
were gone
we sat on your roof
and smoked
our last joint.
it just wasn't fun anymore.
we'd taken the dream
and made
it ordinary.
"we had it all," you said,
"and then
we had to ruin it
by falling in love."

we had it all
and we made one mistake.
we could've lived in a time suspended.
the weightless
the warmth.
but then
we fell in love
and time
started moving again.

the fight of the century.

if you can take
one more hit,
let them hit you.

if the stage is cold
but you can still stand,
let them laugh at you.

if your mom still loves you
after all your shit,
let her hug you.

if your eyes haven't shut
and you can still type,
get one more sentence down.

if you look out the window
and still notice the birds, the sun,
don't jump.

your dog will never stop loving you.
this shouldn't matter,
let her lick you anyway.

if your words sound like rants
and your soul

is still a mystery,
if love started your pilot light
and never took
your god away,
if you have any fight left
then don't sleep
don't stop
don't yawn
don't blink.

there's something they don't tell you about life,
i don't know if it's a curse or a gift
but you've got to own all your time
or someone else will.
don't ever stop swinging
keep sweating
keep bleeding.

the thing about all this is,
once you step out
you can't always
get back into the ring.

the poem.

it's the only thing that feels good
even when you don't get it right.
you made it home
you wrote it.
tomorrow you'll wake up
and no matter what the boss says
and who doesn't show up
and how late they
make you stay,
on the
other end of that city
your words are there.
the hard part
is over -
the poem
is waiting for you.

it's the only thing that feels good
even when you don't get it right.
it's not like sex
or darts
or cooking dinner for your girlfriend.
sometimes it'll be better
but it will never be worse.
it'll wait for you,

grinning
taunting,
forcing you to sharpen your knives
and ambush fleeing words
until you find an answer.

each line brings the light
a little closer.

it's the only thing that feels good
even when you don't get it right.
but sometimes
you do.
those are the rare nights.
the ones that don't even sound true
when you write about them years later.
the ones kids hear
that change their minds,
that maybe it can be them after all,
and they don't have to be
another generation of failures
like the last crop of zombies
who decided they deserved to be parents.

even the artist deserves a victory
every now and then.
sometimes
you get to win
like a rich man.

she's not coming back.

it takes a week after she leaves you.
you haven't changed your underwear in days.
the snake plant is dead and
never coming back.
your only pair of jeans are so crusted
they stand on their own.
and none of those women who tried
to pull you away from your girl
are interested anymore.

it's a wonderful thing to think about
as you come back to life
and like little fireworks
all the philosophies
those poets of the night sang to you
haunt your hangover with no remorse.
the things you agreed with,
the lies you told.
under the bar lights they seemed like gospel.
under the bar lights all the red lips and
smoky eyes look the same.

but the mornings look the same, too.
it's only been a week.
the snake plant is dead.

you're still in the same underwear.
and all the lies you told the night before
can never equal the one truth -
you already had a girl to watch
the end of the world with,
you had found what they were all looking for.

those women with the cocktails
will tell you lots of things
under the bar lights,
things you couldn't imagine coming
from lips like that.
but they won't tell you the only thing
you need to hear: "you could've won."

it takes a hangover to tell you
the things a woman won't.
no matter how bad they hate you
it's nothing like hating yourself.

what is this?

well, here we go again.
it's fall and the garbage piles
don't smell like they have
bodies tied inside.
the french have put away their cameras
and stopped shouting directions
at the old black grandmothers
leaving sunday mass
at mt. olivet church.
"walk out again," they yell. "fix your hat."
too bad the french don't die off
in winter like the mosquitos,
by next spring
they'll have multiplied and found
a new neighborhood
to invade.

but we can finally
leave the windows open.
just in time.
the landlords
jam up traffic on the williamsburg,
crawling over
from crown heights
to turn on the building heat
and boil us for dinner.

two daily bursts of anger are
programmed into the heat pipes
and the one next to the toilet
does the most damage.
maybe it's because i'm around
it before my coffee kicks in
but i always forget and relax,
open a book and
stretch my legs out,
and then any conjunction of
fuck/goddamn/cunt/scum and
sometimes a bunch of
racial slurs with no context
will fly through the apartment
like zealous bats
until my girlfriend yells at me
to "shut up" and "what is that smell?"

the apartment stinks
from the burned skin that falls
off my leg and collects
on the ground like dirty sand.
good thing
my girlfriend's a better vegan
than me.
there are enough bags of peas
in the freezer
to sleep out the pain.

but soon the mice will come
and the roaches will follow.
when the streets get too cold
rent control and locked doors
can't stop instinct.
so we'll shut the windows.
i'll be itchy until may.
my lips will bleed
from the dry heat and i'll say
"we have to get out of new york".
everyone will tell me i'm crazy,
but where else can your half
of the rent be $1,500
and everything is still against you?

what's the point?

no one ever gets what they want.
even when you give a life
your last request
is still too much to ask.
call the grandkids for dinner.
sometimes they'll answer,
and if you catch them off guard
they might just agree to show up.

but never alone.

always with some new asshole
who's trying to get in her pants
or a girlfriend who's tired of hearing
your same stories.
a kid from another generation and time
who'll never know
what it was like to eat out
once a year.
the new american drama played out
in front of your eyes
but instead of normandy
and great depression
it's cell phones and real depression.
you can see it on their faces.

this world.
what is it?
what your first husband
never came back for,
dying alone on some sand so these kids
would never have to know.
what is it?

they can see it on your face.
pop two more sodium pills
and ask the waiter for some water.
he forgets.
the kids are vegans,
you can't even bond over a meal.
they tell you "don't worry" to everything.
you know your son will say no,
but what about the grandkids?
they'll remember the times
you were there to say yes
when their parents
said no.
so you ask them your last request.
a beer.
a final beer.
to have one more glass
of freedom and danger before
the white noise.
and they say no because

it wouldn't be responsible. but
what they really mean is
your happiness
isn't worth the consequences.

so that's it.

but don't worry,
memories are unforgiving.
you'll die soon
but they have their whole lives
to regret
their indifference.

a.d.

the eclipse is coming over the early dawn
of a fallen empire
while stars are revealed
through clouds at high noon
and the horses canter slowly
along an old barbed wire gate.
their hoofs dig new constellations
into forgotten sand
as the hourglass drains faster
to zero
and behind the pastures of torn flags
bluffs crumble against the silent breeze.
we can see it from the north and the south.
but the trail goes cold where
the highway ends
and there's a tide rising
the ancients know
will flood the valley.
new shrines will be etched by the current
that no prophets ever mentioned.
and as the last kid sinks under the surface
a flamingo will float by and drink
from its new backyard,
reaching its head from the water
toward the sky in a mighty gulp
           had always believed
                   world.

Acknowledgements

Joey B, Drew, Christine, Ronald, Kacy, Kyle, Christina Kaylenhart, Mom, Phil, Lauren, Kerri, Paul T & Joe H, Joe La, Josh Dale, Pilleater Leeann B, Ronnie Silva, Mrs. Virgilio, Mr. & Mrs. Burke, Matt Dabson, Sarah E, Brian Weakly, Pablo, Thorns, Andrew D, Jerry Ovad, Jenny Emslie, Rania, Aida, Krista S, Chris A, Chelsey, Adam F, Kaitlin W, Kiley, Zac, Matt Blythe, Sebastian & Lucian, Sean Fodor, V. Vuia, Thirty West, Lil Bil, Chris (48th Street Press), Karina

Made in the USA
San Bernardino, CA
03 April 2018